PERFORMANCE APPRAISAL

One More Time

PERFORMANCE APPRAISAL

One More Time

JOHN D. DRAKE, PH.D.

CRISP PUBLICATIONS

Editor-in-Chief: *William F. Christopher*

Managing Editor: *Kathleen Barcos*

Editor: *Kay Keppler*

Cover Design: *Kathleen Barcos*

Cover Production: *Russell Leong Design*

Book Design & Production: *London Road Design*

Printer: *Bawden Printing*

Library of Congress Card Catalog Number 97-068251

ISBN 1-56052-442-1

For
James C. Cabrera

The first executive to join
Drake Beam Morin, Inc.,
the man who introduced me
to the concept of outplacement,
and a loyal friend. Thanks, Jim.

CONTENTS

Contents

INTRODUCTION

This is a "how to" book. It's all about assembling a performance appraisal (PA) system that will improve performance. However, a good PA system can do a lot more—it can justify salary changes, promotions, and personnel decisions in discrimination lawsuits.

The content is based on many years of trial and error learning. I've seen what has worked and what has not. This book tells it as it is. The result is a rejection of the many costly and complex ideas that have come and gone over the years. This book describes a PA system that gets back to basics, but with a few novel twists.

I believe that the effectiveness of an appraisal system is determined by the quality of communication between the manager and staff member, not by multiple raters, complex scoring methods, or the forms used. If that statement makes sense to you, then you'll find this book a helpful guide. Here's to success with your PA system.

John D. Drake
Kennebunkport, Maine

I.

PERFORMANCE APPRAISAL—
IT'S HERE TO STAY

I F PERFORMANCE APPRAISAL (PA) weren't already in existence, it would quickly be invented. It seems like an appropriate thing to do. If you have employees and want them to perform effectively, you will talk with them about how they're doing their job. You would expect that such a discussion would lead to ways of improving performance.

However, the experience of most managers is that PA rarely improves employees' performance; in fact, sometimes it gets worse. Still, PA efforts continue in almost every organization—mostly because so many reasons exist for employee appraisal: legal documentation, feedback about performance, employee development, corporate planning, salary administration, and more.

The Many Faces
of Performance Appraisal

One can imagine that the earliest PAs were more physical than verbal—the whip provided a clear message about

1

adequacy of performance. During the Industrial Revolution, firing was a common means of communicating work failure. The first industry appraisal appeared in the 1800s in the cotton mills of Scotland. At that time, a multicolored cloth was hung over each person's workstation. Whatever color was turned outward by the supervisor designated the worker's deportment, ranging from excellent to bad. The earliest structured appraisals, as we've come to know them, stemmed from World War I military fitness evaluations. Industrial appraisals slowly began to follow.

Over the past century, employers have tried different approaches to performance appraisal. The question has not been so much about whether PA should be implemented, but rather how to structure it. Among some methods that have been tried:

- Global impressions

- Trait-rating scales

- Performance outcomes

- Behavior-rating scales

- Hybrids (some combination of the above)

> *The sad truth is that, except for one, almost every approach to PA has failed the test of time.*

A Brief Life Cycle

The average corporate PA effort usually lasts about three years. After that time, disappointing results or frustration with its use increases until the dissatisfaction forces a change. Then a new system or program is initiated, only to go through the same cycle until it, too, is dropped.

What is wrong? What can we do about it? These are the questions that the remaining chapters will attempt to answer.

Where We've Been; Where We're Going

PA has a long history because it seems to have much potential. In the 1990s, for example, legal issues relating to discrimination and affirmative action provided additional impetus for its use. Over the years, many kinds of PA approaches have been used, but few have lasted. In most organizations, PA systems have a relatively short life cycle.

The next chapter explores why most PA efforts fail.

II.

Why Such a
Good Idea Can Fail

V ISIT ALMOST ANY ORGANIZATION that has an
established appraisal methodology and ask,
"How satisfied are you with your PA system?"
Most likely, the answers will range from "not very satisfied," to "it's terrible," to a disconcerting, "oh, do we
have one?"

What's the matter? PA systems are usually implemented with good intentions and great thought and planning, but managers can see the underlying difficulties from
these comments gleaned from a recent employee opinion
survey:

> "My boss is a tough rater. My buddy Sam works
> for Eddie—he gives all of his people good ratings.
> It's not fair."

> "I hate it when it's time for me to give performance
> appraisals. It's really uncomfortable to 'play God.' I
> have a strong feeling, too, that my staff dislikes the
> system as much as I do."

"If I put all the time into my work that I put into completing these PA forms, the company would be much further ahead."

"We've got this PA system that computes the salary increases for my people. I know how much each one deserves, but the forms don't take into account some of the factors that are important in making my salary decisions."

These quotes are typical; many employees view their PA system similarly. Listed below are five key reasons why performance appraisal systems rarely work well:

1. They are too threatening

2. They involve too much paperwork

3. Personnel are not adequately trained to provide feedback

4. The PA system is not integrated with other company systems

5. Goals for the PA system are incompatible

Let's examine these issues.

Too Threatening

No one feels comfortable in threatening situations; usually we try to avoid them. PA is no exception. For most employees, fear is present even before the discussion begins. People dislike being judged—especially when the evaluation comes from their boss. Very few employees see the scheduling of a performance review as an upbeat occasion that will help them. Rather, appraisal day is perceived as "judgment day"; anxiety and defensive mechanisms start long before arrival at the boss's office.

The manager does not escape feeling threatened, either. If, during the PA discussion, the manager says something that is interpreted by the employee as a criticism, the employee will become defensive, deny the allegation, and present the story differently. In turn, the manager will react defensively because the "helpful" comment is rejected.

> ➤ *When the psychological defensive mechanisms of manager and employee are in gear, the resulting discussion is almost never productive.*

Defensive Reactions

The boss has an additional discomfort. Most PA efforts require the manager to embark on a kind of parent-child discussion—an uncomfortable role when two adults confer. Robert Lefton, a consultant, describes PA as "the equivalent of walking up to a person and saying, 'Here's what I think of your baby.' It requires knowing how to handle fear, anger, and a gamut of other emotions that a lot of managers aren't comfortable with."

The following segment from a typical PA feedback discussion demonstrates why conducting such appraisals is threatening.

Manager: I think that you need to demand more from your staff.

Employee: I don't know how you can say that. They work damn hard for me.

Manager: I don't mean that they don't work hard, but they've just got to become more productive.

Employee: Look, it's not my fault if our productivity is off a bit. You were the one who turned down my request to let them work overtime. . . .

Can you see where this discussion is headed? Eventually the employee will probably say, "OK, I'll try to push them more." The manager will respond, "Great," but both will know that the employee's commitment to change is probably nil. The reality is that the staff member will say, "What's the use? You bust your back around here and all you get is a kick in the ass. Maybe this isn't the place for me."

The manager will probably also walk away from the appraisal feeling frustrated and disappointed, believing that the interview didn't accomplish much, and concluding that it doesn't pay to be forthright. Any enthusiasm for doing another appraisal is certainly diminished.

➤ *When a PA system requires the manager to judge or criticize, it fosters a climate threatening to both boss and employee. Both seek to avoid the confrontation.*

Too Much Paperwork

"The first step in completing our new appraisal form is to list all of your major job responsibilities. Then in this next section, write down

your objectives for each responsibility for the next rating period. In the third column, indicate the relative importance of each objective."

Imagine the disgust that will greet this task. Unfortunately, such procedures are common. Appraisal forms in many organizations extend to six pages or more.

> ➤ *In part, the paperwork problem can be alleviated by recognizing that different appraisal formats may be needed, depending on the job or organizational level. For example, many organizations include some scale ratings for lower-level jobs, but use narrative formats at managerial levels.*

Reducing Paperwork with Computers

To reduce appraisal writing time, many organizations have placed their PA forms and rating procedures on computers. However, if the questionnaire is lengthy, the expected savings are often unrealized.

Moreover, computerized scoring systems may take the manager's evaluations and use them to calculate summary ratings (scores) over which the appraising manager has no control. These systems are supposed to minimize rater bias, but they send a wrong message. In effect, they say, "We don't trust your objectivity." Small wonder such an approach results in managers investing time in finding ways to beat the system.

> ➤ *Appraisal forms should be tailored to each organization's needs. However, regardless of the approach taken, the rating format needs to be short and easy to use.*

Inadequate Training
for Conducting Reviews

Some organizations don't train their appraisers at all; some distribute a "Performance Appraisal Manual" and assume that it will properly instruct readers; some schedule a briefing on how to complete the rating forms. None of these approaches is adequate.

What training, if any, should companies provide? Kevin Murphy, a psychologist at Colorado State University, offers good insight on this question. He says, "The real problem is not how well managers can evaluate performance, but how willing they are. The problem is one of motivation, not ability."

The motivation to provide feedback is low because most managers feel uncomfortable giving feedback—especially negative feedback. They sense it is risky and tricky; they see themselves as ill-equipped to conduct such discussions.

> ➤ *Organizations should focus more time and effort in training managers on how to conduct appraisal interviews than in trying to improve their rating forms. Managers need to know how to manage the defensiveness and conflict that occurs during many PA feedback discussions.*

Not Integrated into
Other Company Systems

Managers will not embrace a PA system unless they think it will get their job done. If, for example, the PA system is labeled or even perceived as a "program," failure is likely. In such cases, managers will view PA as another chore.

Here are some ways PA can be integrated into a company's way of doing business:

- Objectives and budgets should be interlocked. Objectives (on which the PA is based) should be established at the same time that the organization establishes its annual budget, and where appropriate, integrated with budget requirements.

- Appraisals are conducted at the top as well as the bottom of the organization. PA systems seem more effective when top management sets the example for employees.

- Appraisals are a significant factor in determining salary and advancement (but, as will be discussed in Chapter X, not tied directly to rewards).

- Feedback discussions focus on current work and not personal attributes.

Goals for the Appraisal System Are Not Compatible

> *PA systems fail largely because they are designed with conflicting goals.*

If any organization wants to implement a successful PA system, it needs to recognize the system's limitations. In most cases, an appraisal system cannot accomplish all that is expected of it. This is such an important issue that the entire next chapter is devoted to it.

Where We've Been; Where We're Going

Five key factors lead to disappointing results from appraisal efforts. These include: the system is too threatening, involves too much paperwork, depends on inadequately trained personnel, is not part of other company systems, and has incompatible goals. The most important of these factors is conflicting goals for the PA system. This topic will be explored in our next chapter.

III.

PERFORMANCE APPRAISAL SYSTEMS AND CONFLICTING GOALS

MOST ORGANIZATIONS INITIATE A PA effort to improve productivity. They expect that a systematic way of providing performance feedback is better than leaving such discussions (if any) to the discretion of each supervisor. However, as organizations use their PA system, they gradually want it to do more than improve performance. This list of PA goals is taken from a Fortune 500 company's PA manual:

1.   Improve employee performance

2.   Advise employees as to how their performance is viewed

3.   Encourage employee feedback (upward communication to supervisor)

4.   Provide legal protection (in event of a termination, etc.)

5. Determine salary awards

6. Assist in succession planning

7. Justify promotions

Where's the Conflict?

> *The conflict is simply this: you cannot expect a per-formance appraisal to improve performance when it is also linked directly to rewards (salary or promotion).*

In the list of goals cited by the Fortune 500 company, items 1–4 are attainable in an effectively organized PA system. However, as soon as you add the concept of linking salary or advancement to appraisal (items 5–7), problems arise. Let's see what happens in practice.

Charlie Smith is a plant manager for a major pharmaceutical corporation. At the conclusion of each appraisal, his PA format requires him to rate each employee on a 1–7 scale. He knows from past experience and company policy that it will be almost impossible for him to get any reasonable salary increase for an employee unless he gives a rating of "5" or higher.

One of Charlie's process engineers, Sally Johnson, has been with the company six years. She's a dependable, solid performer, she meets all of Charlie's standards, but she is not out-standing. Last year Charlie's salary budget was cut and he was unable to give increases to several staff members, including Sally.

Figure 1.   Rating to whatever is required
Dilbert reprinted by permission of United Features Syndicate, Inc.

However, because she is a key member of his team and has accumulated extremely valuable process knowledge, he said, "Sally, I'll take care of you next year."

What do you suppose Charlie will do when he makes this year's rating? It's obvious. He'll make the rating come out to whatever is required to get the salary increase he wants for Sally (and others).

Ancillary Problems

The consequences of Charlie's action are many. First, the evaluation will be spuriously high. It won't reflect Sally's true performance.

Second, the inflated rating results in a poor performance appraisal discussion. For the high rating to ring true, Charlie will avoid indicating shortcomings or areas for improvement. Sally will walk away with a distorted vision of Charlie's true assessment of her performance.

Lastly, human resources records will now indicate that Sally "exceeds expectations," a rating that could later come back to haunt the organization should Sally, for example, claim sex discrimination because she was passed over for a promotion. The example of Charlie and Sally is commonplace.

> *Many PA designers fail to foresee that managers will manipulate their appraisals to obtain the salary/promotion desired or to make the PA feedback discussion less threatening.*

Tie Money to Performance Indirectly

Clearly, job performance must be related to rewards. If PA ratings don't have anything to do with salary or advancement, hardly anyone will perceive the PA system as important.

> *The key is that the connection between performance and rewards cannot be direct or mechanical.*

The way in which PA evaluations and salary can be productively related is discussed in Chapter X.

Where We've Been; Where We're Going

A PA system cannot both improve performance and also serve as a vehicle to determine salary or promotions. When rewards are directly linked to the appraisal, significant problems emerge:

1. Managers will distort their ratings so that the numbers yield the salaries they want for their employees.

2. Threat makes the feedback session uncomfortable because both employee and manager know the implications of a low rating. The employee, therefore, is likely to become defensive and conceal problems, much less accept those the boss raises.

3. Little or no performance improvement occurs as a result of the discussion (for the reasons cited in item 2).

The next chapter examines options for measuring performance.

IV.

HOW TO
MEASURE PERFORMANCE

OVER THE YEARS, many methods have been used to measure performance. Most of them can be assigned to one of five basic categories—global impressions, trait-rating scales, behavior-rating scales, performance outcomes, and hybrids. Which works best? To help you decide which is best for your company, let's analyze the options.

Options for Measuring Performance

Global Impressions

These summary ratings use broad categories such as "outstanding" or "moderately satisfactory." Rarely do they spell out specific performance dimensions. Sometimes the global impression is rendered in a paragraph describing the employee's overall performance.

Advantages

1.   Quick—relatively easy to make a rating.

Disadvantages

1.   Employee not likely to understand on which data or performances the ratings are based.

2.   Has limited use for developing employees.

3.   Weak basis for coping with legal issues.

Trait-Rating Scales

Traits are lists of personal qualities. The rater usually indicates on numerical scales the extent to which the employee possesses certain personal qualities such as "dependability," "job cooperativeness," and "initiative."

Advantages

1.   Personal qualities can have relevance to job success.

2.   Ratings can be quickly rendered.

Disadvantages

1.   Do not fare well in legal disputes—difficult to prove linkage between trait and job performance.

2.   Highly vulnerable to error. Rating forms assume manager has observed each of the traits,

even when the rating form includes the option, "Did Not Observe."

3. Arouses strong defensive reactions from employee. Discussion of traits focuses directly on the person rather than the work done.

Behavior-Rating Scales

Employees are rated on the extent to which they display behavior thought to be related to successful performance. Three techniques have been used—the critical incident method, behaviorally based scales, and competencies.

Critical Incident Method. With this technique, the rater must observe the employee and record examples of behavior that strongly contributed to or distracted from good job performance.

Advantages

1. Raters are not forced to attribute traits to employee, but only describe behavior.

Disadvantages

1. A nuisance for managers. Most won't bother to take notes and keep records about incidents.

2. Open to much rater bias. Rater must infer which incidents are critical to job success.

3. Feedback is uncomfortable for most managers. The citation of "negative" incidents arouses

strong defensive reactions. Employees typically claim that the situation was not as the manager observed it.

Behaviorally Anchored Rating Scales (BARS). Managers study jobs to determine which skills or dimensions are important for successful performance (for example, "knowledge of standard accounting methods"). For each job dimension, scales are established that describe a range of behaviors from ideal to poor. These descriptions are usually referred to as behavioral "anchors." Raters then check those anchors that come closest to the employee's behavior. See Figure 2.

Advantages

1. Few inferences are required of rater—appraisal is based on some form of job analysis.

2. Effective for legal defenses—ratings based on specific job-relevant dimensions.

Disadvantages

1. Requires considerable research effort to develop job dimensions and behavioral anchors.

2. Can become outdated as jobs and organizations change.

3. Despite a seemingly scientific approach, has the same vulnerability to rating errors as trait methods.

Position: Chemical Equipment Operator
Job Dimension: Verbal Communication

7

This operator could be expected to:
check verbal instructions against written procedures, always check to make sure he heard others correctly, brief his replacements quickly and accurately, giving only relevant information.

6

This operator could be expected to:
inform superiors immediately if problems arise, listen to others carefully and ask questions if he does not understand, give information, instructions, etc., in calm, clear voice.

5

This operator could be expected to:
always inform others of his location in the plant, avoid discussing non-work related subjects when relating plant status to others, inform others of all delays that took place on the shift.

4

This operator could be expected to:
give others detailed account of what needs to be done, but not to establish priorities, mumble when speaking to others, not face the person communicating with him and act disinterested.

3

This operator could be expected to:
fail to relate all necessary details to those relieving him at break or shift change, not seek information and only offer it when asked, guess at status of vessels when relaying information, not check to be sure he has heard others correctly but rely on what he thought he heard, leave out information about his own errors when talking to others.

2

This operator could be expected to:
never ask for help if unsure of something or if errors are made, refuse to listen to others, continually yell at others and use abusive language.

1

This operator could be expected to:
not answer when he is called, refuse to brief his replacements, give person relieving him inaccurate information deliberately.

R. Beatty/C. Schneier, *Personnel Administration* (page 129). © 1981 Addison-Wesley Publishing Company, Inc. Reprinted by permission of Addison Wesley Longman, Inc.

Figure 2. **Example of a behaviorally anchored rating scale**

Competencies.   Competencies are factors believed to distinguish successful and unsuccessful employees. Organizationwide competencies are often referred to as *core competencies* because they support the organization's mission or values. Figure 3 shows an example of a core competency ("Customer Service") and its underlying competencies for appraising employees.

Advantages

1.   Based on studies of requirements for successful performance.

2.   Can help focus attention on behavior that supports organizational priorities.

Disadvantages

1.   Costly and time-consuming to develop.

2.   Cumbersome to change as conditions change.

3.   Subject to same defensive reactions as with traits.

Performance Outcomes

Unlike behaviorally based scales that focus on job behaviors, performance evaluations rate outcomes—what the employee produces in performing the job. Performance is appraised by the extent to which the employee attains certain goals or objectives.

How well does this person perform this competency?
Please use the following scale for your evaluation:

(9–10) An Exceptional Skill. This individual consistently exceeds behavior and skills expectations in this area.

(7–8) A Strength. This individual meets most and exceeds some of the behavior and skills expectations in this area.

(5–6) Appropriate Skill Level. The individual meets a majority of the behavior and skills expectations in this area for this job. There is generally a positive perspective toward responsibilities.

(3–4) Not a Strength. The individual meets some behavior and skills expectations in this area but sometimes falls short.

(1–2) Least Skilled. The individual consistently fails to reach behavior and skills expectations in this area.

(N) "Not Applicable" or "Not Observed"

Customer Service

Treats customers like
business partners   N 1 2 3 4 5 6 7 8 9 10

Identifies, understands,
and responds to appropriate
needs of customers   N 1 2 3 4 5 6 7 8 9 10

Presents ideas simply and clearly   N 1 2 3 4 5 6 7 8 9 10

Listens actively to internal and
external customers   N 1 2 3 4 5 6 7 8 9 10

Solicits and provides constructive
and honest feedback   N 1 2 3 4 5 6 7 8 9 10

Keeps others informed   N 1 2 3 4 5 6 7 8 9 10

Balances requests with business
requirements   N 1 2 3 4 5 6 7 8 9 10

*Figure 3.   Example of a performance
appraisal form using competencies*

Advantages

1. Perceived as relevant and job-related. Relatively easy for managers to support the system.

2. Lends itself to job development and personal growth.

3. Not time-consuming or costly to set up.

4. Has been successful in improving performance.

5. Useful for legal defense.

Disadvantages

1. Difficult to apply when employee has little control over outcomes.

Hybrid Systems

Hybrid appraisal systems base performance ratings on a combination of factors. They try to make up for weaknesses in one approach by adding dimensions of another. For example, BARS is responsive to administrative needs (categorical scoring), whereas performance-based ratings are usually most helpful for developing employees. Using these two kinds of ratings attempts to fill both needs.

Advantages

1. Can meet a broader range of PA goals than a single rating system.

2. Can combine the advantages of several systems.

Disadvantages

1. Depending on the combination selected, could be costly to design, introduce, and implement.

2. Could be seen as overkill; i.e., too much of a burden for managers.

What Conclusions Can We Draw?

No performance measure is ideal. All performance measures have some value, but many have inherent problems that severely limit their effectiveness. Combining approaches might help to overcome the limitation of any individual system. However, as more elements are added to the appraisal system, problems of expense and managerial acceptance quickly emerge.

Performance-based ratings—job objectives—still represent the best vehicle for discussing job behavior and improving productivity. Even in organizations that have found their objective-based PA systems to be ineffective, the failure can almost always be traced to the misuse of objectives.

Where We've Been; Where We're Going

Of all the ways to measure performance, for most organizations the goal/objectives method represents the best vehicle for evaluating performance and obtaining job improvement.

The next chapter explores how to use objectives to bring about improved performance.

V.

USING OBJECTIVES TO IMPROVE PERFORMANCE

ARENʼT OBJECTIVES OLD-FASHIONED? Yes, of course they are. Theyʼve been around ever since Peter Drucker introduced the concept of management by objectives. MBO has lasted because planning and setting goals are how most businesses are run.

Although an objective-based PA system is a goal for every business activity, insufficient training on discussing and establishing these objectives can cause failures. Objectives seem to work best when they are:

- Set by the employee; approved by the manager

- Few rather than many

- Changed as conditions change

- Used when the incumbent can influence the outcome

- Job-related, not personal judgments

- Reviewed frequently

- Written specifically

Let's discuss them, one by one.

Set by the Employee; Approved by the Manager

Setting objectives works only when employees are motivated and committed to complete them. Obviously, if I establish goals for myself, I'm likely to generate ones I believe I can achieve. More importantly, prior mutual agreement on objectives permits easy discussion of progress. This element is critical for successful PA efforts.

> ➤ *Before staff members establish their objectives,*
> *the manager should provide the direction or focus*
> *toward which staff goals should be oriented. Ideally,*
> *this thrust also supports the organization's priorities.*

For example, a manager may say to the staff: "This year, one of my key objectives is to improve our customer service. As you develop your objectives, please keep this focus in mind."

Some issues:

1. *Employees may set easy-to-attain goals to insure a high rating.* If they do, and if goals are not adequate, the boss can challenge the staff member to reach for more. If more is not forthcoming, the manager can insist. After all, the manager is responsible for the output of the unit. In a perfect world, both manager and employee agree on the goals, but sometimes they can't.

2. *Employees may set unrealistically high objectives.* Individual psychological issues affect goal setting. With some employees, managers may have to go along with employees' "overreach" objectives because past experience has shown that these persons need to be challenged to reach an acceptable level of achievement. For other staff members, the goals may need to be softened.

➤ *The prime consideration for determining how tough or easy an employee's objectives should be is the* results *that the selected goals are likely to produce.*

The lesson here is that established objectives rest with the judgment of the manager. Arbitrary guidelines are almost always ineffectual.

Few Rather than Many

I have seen PA systems in which participants listed as many as 25 objectives (usually because they were required to write objectives for all the responsibilities in their job description). Who wouldn't resist such a system?

What is few? Well, it depends. There is no magic number. As you go lower in the organization, the number of job objectives usually increases (smaller, more specific tasks); the number also increases if the organization or job environment is rapidly changing.

➤ *A good criterion for determining whether a particular objective should be included in the PA system is to ask, "Would this objective be worth discussing during the year?" If the answer is "no," eliminate it.*

For most upper-level positions, six objectives are usually sufficient; at middle management, ten are ample. The chairman of the board may have only one—"By end of FY, increase earnings per share by 10%."

Changed as Conditions Change

Amazingly enough, some organizations adopt the mentality that "these are your objectives and that's what you'll be judged against, come hell or high water." Change is ever present. The economy changes, marketplaces change, suppliers change, companies reorganize, shrink, and change in limitless ways.

If staff members are held accountable for objectives that are no longer attainable for reasons beyond their control, it doesn't make much sense to hold them to those objectives. A common argument in support of fixed objectives is that it "evens out"—some become harder; some become easier. Of course, such thinking assumes perfect objectivity on everyone's part. It fails to account for negative feelings that emanate from being judged on criteria that are unrealistic. Such rigidity only leads to alienation from the appraisal system.

> ➤ *An effective PA system provides the means, between the time the objectives are established and the summary appraisal, to adjust goals as conditions warrant. The boss always has the option of keeping the objectives firm, but wiser managers will be flexible and not let the system override good judgment.*

Used When the Incumbent Can Influence the Outcome

If this section's title weren't already lengthy, we might have tacked on, "and yield measurable results." In a word, objectives-based appraisals work best as a function of organizational level—they are more effective at upper and middle management/professional levels than with nonexempts. At the lowest levels, especially in automated production settings, objectives-based appraisals are inappropriate.

> ➤ *Organizations should consider two or three PA formats, each one tailored to the organizational level or job content.*

Job-Related, Not Personal Judgments

Personal qualities (dependability, for example) and behavioral patterns are important. *How* someone performs the job does have significance. The question is, "Does discussion of personal qualities or behaviors lead to improved performance?" Experience answers, "Hardly ever."

> ➤ *Improvement doesn't occur often enough to be worth the price of making appraisal of behavior a key part of your PA system.*

The discussion of personal qualities or behavior patterns creates problems in PA systems for several reasons. First, such an approach arouses defensiveness. I can talk about my job accomplishments or failures relatively easily—success or failure is something I do, but it's not me. Once you focus on the individual, however, you're stepping on sensitive ground. Most people have a strong need to protect their egos.

Here's a typical example.

Boss: . . . and on this competency, "keeps others informed," I rated you as "needs improvement."

Bill: I don't understand that. I attend all the meetings and I think I participate as much as anybody.

Boss: It's not so much the formal meetings I'm talking about, Bill, it's keeping me and others on the team more informed about how things are going with your group and your customers.

Bill: Well, maybe I don't socialize as much as the others and just drop by to chat, but I've been busy with my staff and customers. As you know, I've got good relations with our customers and I'm well over my quota. Are you displeased with how my work is going?

Boss: Oh no, Bill, you've been doing a great job. It's just that I thought . . .

Another reason for not rating behavior in PA systems is that most people change only with great difficulty. First, they have to accept that they have a problem. Then they have to perceive the problem as sufficiently important to do something about it. Last, they must have the where-withal—the skills, insights, help, etc., to make the change. The likelihood of all these conditions being present, and hence the employee making a behavioral change, is low.

Should manager and employee ever talk about behavior?

Yes, of course. *Behavior should be discussed whenever it interferes with getting the job done.* But the time and place are important. The best and most productive time to discuss behavior is when progress on the employee's objectives is under review. In the example below, notice how a job-objective discussion leads naturally to talking about behavior.

> *Cliff:* On this objective, "complete software design for the new warehouse inventory system by Sept. 14," I'm afraid that we won't make the deadline.

> *Boss:* I knew you were a little behind. What seems to be the problem?

(Note how easy it was for Cliff's boss to get the conversation into a problem-solving mode. In this case, it led to a behavioral issue.)

> *Cliff:* I'm having trouble getting the data from the warehouse staff. They still haven't sent me all that we requested.

> *Boss:* I'm surprised. They're usually quite cooperative.

> *Cliff:* Well, maybe for you they are, but not for me.

> *Boss:* How did you approach them?

> *Cliff:* I called them a couple of times; I thought that what I did was fine. But you know the pressure we're under; maybe I came on a little strong.

Boss: That's an interesting thought. I've noticed that when you're under pressure you tend to get a bit impatient—maybe a little abrupt. Do you think that could have happened with the warehouse people?

Cliff: Yeah, it's possible. Maybe I better mend some fences and talk with them again.

Reviewed Frequently

After objectives are mutually agreed upon (or as close to mutually as possible) and before the summary review, progress toward goals should be discussed. In most cases, this procedure is relatively nonthreatening; it usually involves the employee reporting on how much or little progress has been made toward achieving the objectives.

> ➤ *Improvement in performance usually results from progress reviews—not end-of-the-year summary reviews.*

The frequency of these progress reviews depends on the time frames of the objectives and how rapidly conditions are changing. For most upper and middle managers, quarterly progress reviews seem adequate. Such reviews can coincide with the availability of quarterly financial statements. At lower levels, monthly or bimonthly reviews may be more beneficial.

Ultimately, it should be left to the manager's discretion to determine how frequently progress reviews will be profitable. Most good managers use progress reviews as the key element in the management of their staff.

Written Specifically

Successful use of objectives requires that they be written specifically. When goals are specific, progress and summary reviews become much more comfortable for the manager to conduct. Managers will find, for example, that arguments about whether or not an objective was achieved become minimal.

Specific objectives have these characteristics:

1. Focus on end results

2. Have a target date for completion

3. Are expressed in quantitative or categorical terms

4. Specify maximum cost factors

For example: Upgrade all 200 customer service networked computers to Windows NT by end of FY at a cost not to exceed $200,000.

I have often heard that not all objectives can be quantified. Maybe not. But, consider this:

> ➤ *Almost every goal can be made unambiguous by answering the question, "How will we know this goal is accomplished—what will the end result be?"*

A look at a fictitious consultant/client discussion may help us understand how the end result concept works:

Client: Here's one for you. I've got an employee who really doesn't write well. I'd like this employee to work on that as a developmental objective, but I'll be damned if I can see how to quantify it.

Consultant: What is it you're seeing that leads to the "poor writing" conclusion?

Client: It seems like almost every day I'm sending a report back to be corrected for grammar or spelling errors.

Consultant: If the employee improves, what end results would you like to see?

Client: That's easy. I'd like to find that I don't have to send so many reports back for correction.

Consultant: What would be good—how many?

Client: None would be ideal, but realistically, I'd be happy if I only had to send one or two back each month.

Consultant: What would be a reasonable amount of time for him to make that kind of progress?

Client: If he could improve that much in three months, I'd be satisfied.

Consultant: There you have it: "Improve writing skills so that by March 1 (three months from today) no more than two items per month are returned for grammar corrections."

Client: You left out the cost dimension. I'd be willing to approve a company tuition grant for a course on English grammar or writing, let's say up to $500.

Consultant: You're right. OK, the new, quantified objective now reads: *"Improve writing skills so that by March 1, no more than two items per month are returned for correction, at a cost not to exceed $500 tuition."*

Here's another brief example.

Not Specific: Study alternative methods of acquiring the 40-acre parcel adjacent to our Bangor plant.

Specific: Submit written report to VP Finance by Sept. 15 with your recommendation and other possible options for the most cost-effective method of acquiring the 40-acre parcel next to our Bangor plant. Costs to prepare the recommendation are not to exceed $2,000.

➤ *When objectives are specific, the employee, as well as the manager, can tell whether or not the goal was accomplished. This permits an atmosphere of trust to emerge; both parties can now examine the situation with a problem-solving mentality.*

The words "We both thought we could achieve this goal, what seems to be the problem?" come easily and naturally. In this kind of discussion environment, the possibility exists for the conversation to turn to ways of improving less-than-satisfactory performance.

Where We've Been; Where We're Going

This chapter described seven factors for effective use of job objectives:

1. Set by the employee; approved by the manager

2. Few rather than many

3. Changed as conditions change

4. Used when the incumbent can influence the outcome

5. Job-related, not personal judgments

6. Reviewed frequently

7. Written specifically

When objectives are used in this manner, they establish an environment in which constructive discussion can ensue. These discussions—progress reviews—often lead to improved performance.

The next chapter will provide a model for establishing a PA system that works.

VI.

PERFORMANCE APPRAISAL
THAT WORKS

A PA SYSTEM "WORKS" WHEN the organization doesn't constantly fight it and when most of its purposes are attained. It's unrealistic to think every employee will feel positive or be helped by your PA system. Stephen Harper, a professor of management at the University of North Carolina, put it this way: "Performance review will never be a panacea for organizational ills and it will never be free of problems, but until we find something to replace it, managers must learn to use it in the most constructive way." The essential question is: how do you get managers to use the organization's PA system in a constructive way?

What It Takes

> *For managers to embrace any PA system, they must find it useful—they need to see a direct payoff for their efforts. That means that things get done better, faster, or with less effort as a result of using the system.*

No matter how sophisticated the system, no matter what pains are taken to eliminate appraiser bias, a PA system will not work if managers see it as an activity that interferes with doing whatever else they judge as more important.

Managers will find a PA system useful to the extent that it has eight key characteristics. These include:

1. Organization declares "improved performance" as the system's primary goal

2. Integrated with other company systems (such as budgets)

3. Easy to accomplish; involves minimal paperwork

4. Supported by solid training in job coaching (PA feedback)

5. Linked to rewards and promotions, but not directly

6. Provides a sound basis for defense against discrimination allegations

7. Relatively nonthreatening

8. Free of any form of quantitative rating

Yes, you read item 8 correctly—"free of any form of quantitative rating." The next few chapters will elaborate on the rationale for this criterion. It represents the next step in PA's evolutionary cycle.

What a Working System Looks Like

Basically, a working PA system is a hybrid system, but not hybrid in the usual sense (that is, having two rating formats such as traits and competencies). Instead, here hybrid means a two-part system—one for performance, another for salary or rewards.

The performance improvement part consists of three simple stages:

Stage 1—Work Planning

Stage 2—Progress Reviews

Stage 3—Summary Appraisal

The reward part of our recommended PA system is designed to meet the organization's administrative needs. It is distinct and separate from the three performance improvement stages and may or may not be reviewed with the employee.

Conceptually, the model looks like the one pictured in Figure 4.

The PA system described in this figure is not a once-a-year event. Rather, it is a year-long process that starts with work planning.

Work Planning

Planning is essential because it lets employees know the appraisal standards. These standards—goals or objectives—also set the stage for subsequent, relatively non-threatening discussions about the employee's progress toward their attainment.

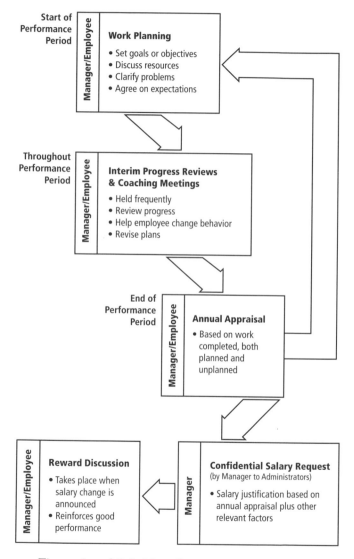

Figure 4. A hybrid performance appraisal model

Progress Reviews

These discussions are the heart of this PA system. They give the manager an opportunity to coach and influence the employee's work efforts; they help ensure that goals set during work planning are met. In this segment of the PA system, managers find the payoff for their efforts—more goals are met as a consequence of progress reviews than if no PA system were in place.

Summary Appraisal

This interview recapitulates all that has taken place throughout the performance period. It is *not* a time for coaching or efforts at improving performance. Rarely, if ever, do annual appraisals result in improved performance. It is an occasion for managers to describe their perspective on how well each employee has met the established goals.

Salary/Reward Recommendation

Recommendations for rewards are best kept separate from any discussion about performance, because most managers consider other factors (in addition to performance) when deciding an employee's salary. A competitive job offer and the employee's potential are two examples. These and other relevant factors should be included in any salary recommendation process. In the PA system proposed, the justifications for salary changes do not need to be shared with the employee.

The performance/rewards link of our PA system shall be fully explored in Chapter X. In the meantime, let's see how to put the performance improvement segments in operation.

The PA system as described represents the component steps for effectively managing the work of others. The system is useful because it sets up a practical, job-centered flow of communication.

Simple? Yes. Easy? Relatively so. Different? Well, yes. Once you eliminate a quantitative rating, the system's non-traditional nature emerges.

> ➤ *Eliminating quantitative ratings makes an incredible difference in the climate of any discussion about performance. It is the key to constructive discussions about work accomplishments.*

What's New?

The PA model proposed here is similar to that suggested in 1957 by Douglas McGregor and further refined in 1965 by Meyer, Kay, and French. It reappears here because it has stood the test of time. It makes sense: the underlying concepts are psychologically sound; they fit today's team-oriented, employee-empowered organizations.

What is new is that we have eliminated judgmental ratings and the complicated rating/feedback schemes that have proliferated since 1957. This model is not costly to implement or sustain. It works because it parallels the way effective managers work.

Fitting in Today's Organizations

Today's organizations are different than when McGregor was writing about them, but not in ways that make application of this employee-centered PA model inappropriate. For example, participative management styles are far more prevalent in today's corporations than in 1957. At that time, the idea of employees setting their own objectives was radical.

On the other hand, today's organizations differ in their hierarchical structure: wider spans of control sometimes make it difficult for the manager to observe individual performance; matrix and project management structures often result in less employee interaction with the boss. The same is true in organizations making extensive use of work teams. Some would even argue that a one-rater system won't work anymore.

While some organizational structures make it difficult for the manager to have a complete picture of an employee's performance, it's not impossible to do so. The manager might have to solicit information from others to do a good assessment. However, the gathering of additional information is best left to each individual manager and not with complex, multi-rater methods such as 360° feedback.*

Multi-rater techniques may help minimize bias and provide evaluations from a broader perspective, but the evidence does not show that employees will accept or react positively to such feedback. Carefully constructed interviews between managers and their employees are still needed if feedback is to be accepted.

*See Deborah Jude-York and Susan L. Wise, *Multipoint Feedback: A 360° Catalyst for Change* (Menlo Park, CA: Crisp Publications, 1997).

Multiple Raters—A Tempting Trap

PA system designers need to know that when multiple raters are added to a PA format, the system becomes more complicated—a condition that usually leads to its early demise. Systematic use of multiple raters often requires the design of sophisticated rating formats, the collection and collating of ratings, and means of preserving rater anonymity.

Although feedback from several sources may enrich the input about the employee's performance, it does not ensure that the employee will act on it. Working through defenses and accepting responsibility for problems is still best accomplished in one-on-one discussions with the boss. Here's a fairly typical example:

> On reading a profile report from anonymous assessors (peers and others), Debbie noted that her ratings were above average, except for "supports team goals." On this competency, she received a "below average" score. This was Debbie's reaction: "Sure they rated me that way—Sally and I were the only ones who met our sales quotas. If they had spent more time paying attention to customers instead of having so many meetings, they wouldn't be trying to stick it to me."

Just as corporations are finding it profitable to divest diverse operations and focus on their core businesses, so too, it's time to get back to basics on PA systems. Over the past few decades we've put so much effort into attempting to eliminate rater bias that we have diverted our attention from the core issue—helping the employee change in ways to improve performance.

> ➤ *Changed behavior does not stem from improved rating forms or multiple raters; it changes when well-trained managers coach their employees in a problem-solving atmosphere.*

Where We've Been; Where We're Going

This chapter presented a model for establishing a PA system that managers might find useful. For a PA system to bring about improved performance, eight important conditions were specified. These factors help create a PA system that is simple to use and relatively nonthreatening.

A PA model incorporating the eight conditions was presented. It represents a return to basics that fits with today's empowered employees. Its focus is on manager/employee coaching discussions that embody these elements:

1. Performance discussions are based on mutually established goals.

2. Progress toward these goals is discussed frequently during the rating period.

3. A summary appraisal is provided at the end of the rating cycle, but no quantitative evaluation is rendered.

The next chapter shows how to implement the model; you will be given techniques and methods for conducting productive performance discussions.

VII.

MAKING FEEDBACK
DISCUSSIONS PRODUCTIVE

W
HATEVER FEEDBACK DESIGN YOU SELECT, four basic principles should be considered when setting up your system: specific, immediate, descriptive rather than evaluative, and two-way.

Specific

Staff members like it when the boss says they've done a good job, but such feedback is more meaningful (and thus more likely to reinforce good job behavior) when the manager also specifies exactly what was liked about the performance.

Gift giving provides a good analogy. If you give Janet a sweater for her birthday and she says, "Thank you, I really like it," you may wonder if she is saying that merely because she is compelled to say something positive or because she truly appreciates it. On the other hand, if Janet explains specifically *why* she likes it, her response is far more meaningful. Compare this answer to her first statement: "I really like this sweater; it will go perfectly with a blue skirt I have. Wait a minute, I'll get it and show you—the two together will make a great outfit!"

Here's a performance appraisal example.

Not Specific: You're good at meeting deadlines.

Specific: I like it very much when you have all the cost reports to me two or three days before the monthly budget meeting. It gives me a good opportunity to organize my presentation.

After receiving such specific, positive feedback, the employee probably will want to continue the affirmed behavior. The same specificity principle applies to negative feedback. We'll discuss this in greater detail when we describe how to make feedback descriptive.

Immediate

"Immediate" may be too strong a word. Obviously, managers cannot always provide instant feedback. Still, feedback should occur as close to the event as possible. If the boss says, "Remember last year when . . . ," the employee's reaction (verbalized or not) is likely to be, "Why didn't you tell me then, when I could have done something about it?"

> ➤ *Timely feedback is one of the major reasons for having frequent progress reviews.*

Descriptive

"Descriptive" means to describe results or behavior rather than to state a value judgment. When negative feedback is evaluative, it is almost always perceived as a criticism. As a result, employees respond with ego-protecting efforts; that is, they get defensive and reject the feedback.

For example:

> *Boss:* With all of your people leaving, I have to question the strength of your management skills.

> *Fred:* It wasn't my fault they left. You told me to push my people and do whatever it took to get the work done on schedule. I did exactly what you suggested.

The examples listed demonstrate the difference between descriptive and evaluative. In each of these examples, the manager gets the point across. However, one method works better than the other.

> ➤ *In the evaluative approach the* employee *is attacked or accused; in the descriptive method the* event *or* situation *is the focus.*

Evaluative	Descriptive
"You don't plan well."	"When you plan, I notice you put together a weekly schedule, but not a monthly list of priorities."
"You did a poor job in conducting the team meeting this morning."	"I would like to talk with you about the team meeting this morning and, in particular, about what happened when participants began directing their questions to me rather than to you."

Two-Way

Productive feedback discussions almost always require
the boss to take responsibility for making the conversation
two-way. Without hearing the employee's reaction to what
is said, the manager does not learn whether the feedback
is accepted. Moreover, employees often need time to process feedback to assimilate and accept it. This process is
facilitated by encouraging staff members to share their
thoughts and feelings as the appraisal progresses.

Where We've Been; Where We're Going

This chapter pointed out that feedback is constructive and helpful to the extent that it is specific, immediate,
descriptive, and two-way. Judgmental, negative feedback
spawns strong defensive reactions, which can be reduced
significantly by describing the issue rather than evaluating
the person.

The next chapter will focus on the best ways to man-
age the difficult task of giving your employee negative
feedback.

VIII.

WHEN YOU GIVE
NEGATIVE FEEDBACK

S OONER OR LATER, the manager will need to explain to an employee that something is wrong–that something is not being done properly. No matter how the statement is worded, it will be perceived as criticism and engender defensive reactions such as arguing, being silent, psychologically withdrawing, or falsely acquiescing ("You're right, it's all my fault").

> *Whenever an employee is confronted with an issue that implies failure, some defensiveness will occur. The manner in which the manager handles this defensiveness is the critical, make-or-break point in any PA feedback discussion.*

Steps for Providing Negative Feedback

By following the procedures suggested by our six-step model, most managers can help their employees move past their defensive reactions and objectively examine the issue. Here are the steps:

1. Describe the problem

2. Listen

3. Get agreement on the problem

4. Involve employee in determining solutions

5. Ask employee to summarize

6. Set follow-up date

Step 1.
Describe the Problem

Remember that managers can present their thoughts descriptively rather than evaluatively. To help keep negative judgments out of the boss's comments, focus on:

- What happened (or was observed)

- Who was involved

- How frequently it occurred

- The effect it had

For example:

I'm sorry, Tom, but I can't agree with your conclusion that this objective has been satisfactorily completed. Your report was submitted before the deadline, but when you presented your findings at the quality meeting, Susy, Bill, and Jennifer strongly objected to your proposed changes in the sampling procedure. It does not appear that our team follows the new procedures.

Step 2.
Listen

When the employee reacts defensively, usually by responding with excuses or explanations, the manager must not argue back. Instead, at this moment, the manager must try to understand the employee's point of view. When such a procedure is not followed, the discussion becomes counterproductive. Here's an example:

Words Spoken	Action Taken
Manager: Chris, the cost reports have been late for the past two weeks.	Describing the problem
Chris: Well, we had two people out sick with the flu—it's been a rough week.	Explains/justifies position
Manager: I know that makes it tough, but those reports are really needed on time. Why didn't you put some of your staff on overtime?	Rejects Chris's explanation
Chris: A couple of them did work overtime, but you know the push we've had to keep payroll down.	More justification; hostility creeping in

Manager: You should have let me know you were in a bind—I could have gotten you some help from the purchasing department.	Further attack. Denies Chris's explanation
Chris: I never thought of that.	Defense by retreating
Manager: Well, that's what I'm here for—to be of help.	Further attack
Chris: Bob will be in on Thursday and I think Sally can make it by Friday. We'll have the report on time next week, OK?	Defensive. I'll be cooperative and get the boss off my back.
Manager: Thanks, Chris. It's important to get these reports to me on time.	Further attack

What is Chris's attitude as he leaves this discussion? Did he find the feedback helpful? Will he be more willing to share problems with his boss in the future?

While some managers might consider the above dialogue successful, the failure to listen and express understanding of the employee's viewpoint merely results in time spent by *both* parties adjusting their defenses. Neither the manager nor Chris focused on the problem in a constructive way. Conceptually, the typical boss-employee confrontation follows this pattern.

Boss: Says or describes something the employee has done less than satisfactorily

Employee: Responds defensively—explains or justifies position

Boss: Disagrees or rejects explanation ("Yes, but . . .")

Employee: Becomes more defensive. Offers additional explanations; may becomes antagonistic or silent.

➤ *Employees cannot focus on the boss's comments when they are busy defending themselves. To focus attention on the issue, the manager must avoid the "Yes, but . . ." response and make the decision to listen.*

It is beyond the scope of this book to describe listening techniques, but the key tools at the manager's disposal are:

* *Accepting.* Neither approve nor disapprove. For example, "I see," "I understand," "uh huh."

* *Restating Content.* Mirror, in your own words, the meaning of what is said. For example:

  Employee: I'm trying hard to meet this objective, but our software really isn't up to the challenge.

  Manager: I see. The problem is really a matter of your not being able to process the data.

* *Reflect Feelings or Attitudes.* Reflecting feelings is similar to restating except that you do not restate the spoken words, but show an understanding of the revealed emotions.

> *Employee:* That damn second shift fouled me up again!
>
> *Manager:* You're really angry about it.

- *Ask Open-Ended Questions.* These do not lend themselves to "yes" or "no" responses. For example:

  What do you think we can do about the problem?

  How can I help you with this?

- *Silence.* Don't misuse this tactic. This tool can be most effectively used immediately after the manager asks a question. The principle is this: when you ask a question, do not speak next.

Restating—A Most Valuable Tool. Restating is the most helpful of the listening techniques as an immediate response to the employee's initial justification or excuse. Restating helps keep the boss from arguing and therefore rejecting the employee's side of the story. Secondly, restating creates a climate that encourages the employee to elaborate on the situation.

As employees hear their own words mirrored back, they often take a second look at what has been said. Staff members may realize, for example, that what was said wasn't exactly the entire story or that it didn't come across in the way it was intended.

Here's an example from a manager-employee conflict discussion in which the manager avoided an argument by restating.

Manager: Rich, this is the third time this week you've been late. (Descriptive statement)

Rich: I couldn't help it. With this bad weather and snow, I've been held up in traffic. It's terrible.

Manager: Let's see what you're saying here . . . the reason you've been late these past few mornings is the traffic tie-ups. (The manager, although tempted, did not argue with Rich's excuses by saying, "Well, Rick, I drove almost the same route and made it here on time. Traffic wasn't that bad.")

Rich: Well, it's kinda tough getting out of the house on time . . . it's not always easy.

Manager: (Still withholding judgment and trying to understand) Some things at home in the morning are making it difficult, too.

Rich: I didn't want to say anything, but, frankly, I've got a few problems with my son.

Manager: It sounds like it's difficult to talk about.

Rich: I guess I might as well tell you. My teenager is rebelling against going to school and . . .

The Problem with Arguing. Very little is gained by stripping away an employee's excuses. It is more important to create a climate in which the staff member stops being defensive and begins to explore the problem.

Think of it this way: as long as the manager attacks the employee's defenses (excuses or justifications), the employee will continue to rebuild them. However, once the manager allows the employee to save face, the employee no longer needs to expend energy in self-defense and can now examine the issues.

Reducing Defensiveness by Exploring Feelings. One of the listed listening techniques was "reflect feelings or attitudes." For many managers, this approach may appear to be an awkward measure for combating defensiveness. However, negative feedback stirs strong emotions—feelings of pain, anger, or fear. Releasing these feelings can be very beneficial.

> ➤ *Whenever emotions govern behavior, objective conversation is unlikely. After any criticism, therefore, managers should ask employees how they* feel *about what was said.*

Inquiring about feelings is particularly helpful when the manager senses that the discussion is fruitless. Here is an example:

Suppose a manager expresses disappointment about an objective that an employee failed to meet. As the topic is mentioned, the employee reacts by gazing at the floor and mumbling brief, uncommunicative sentences. Instead of focusing on the problem, the employee seems to be retreating from the discussion.

Assuming that the manager has tried to listen and has not rejected the employee's justifications, discussion of feelings is now appropriate. It might go like this:

Manager: Andy, we've been talking here about an unmet objective, but we're not really focusing on the problem or how we can resolve it. Tell me, how do you feel about my bringing up the topic of the missed deadline?

Andy: I think that . . .

Manager: Andy, I'm interested more in how you *feel* and not just what you think. Are you angry, are you sad, are you happy, what? How do you feel about my asking about this unfinished objective?

Andy: Oh, "feel." Well, I guess I feel discouraged about it.

Manager: Why do you feel discouraged?

Andy: You probably don't remember this, but about a year ago we were discussing the performance of my department, and you talked about the importance of being realistic with our time lines. And, you know, this past year I can't think of one situation that we haven't delivered, on schedule, what we said we would. Now with this review I'm late with one objective and you're chewing me out about it. So if you wonder why I'm discouraged, that's why.

Manager: Andy, I'm so sorry. You're right. I should
have recognized your accomplishments. You
have done a great job during the year . . .

Notice that Andy's feelings of discouragement
blocked any constructive communication. By encouraging
Andy to share his feelings, the manager uncovered the
difficulty and was able to take action.

Imagine, on the other hand, if the manager had
not asked for feelings. Suppose she has reemphasized the
importance of completing objectives on time. We can visu-
alize Andy eventually saying, "I know you're right; I'll try
to make certain it doesn't happen again." While these
words sound as though the manager has made progress,
more likely they are said simply to appease the boss. Andy
probably wouldn't change his behavior.

> ➤ *You must listen to your employee's side of the story.*
> *Rejecting your employee's defenses leads to more*
> *defensiveness. On the other hand, don't agree with*
> *an excuse you don't believe. If you can't disagree*
> *or agree, the only remaining option is to listen!*

If you listen to your employee's viewpoint, three
outcomes are likely:

1. Employees may perceive that some of their
    excuses were not valid—that they themselves
    were partly to blame for the problem. In such
    cases, the manager can move on to Step 3,
    "Get Agreement on the Problem."

2.	You may learn that you were wrong. In such cases, you can save yourself the embarrassment of holding an incorrect position.

3.	There could be a standoff. Your employee does not accept any blame for the problem but continues to make excuses or display defensive behavior. When this occurs, initiate a discussion of feelings. More often than not, this procedure will dissolve the stalemate.

Step 3.
Get Agreement on the Problem

Once it is clear that an objective has not been met, most employers seek a solution. In a desire to convert the interview into practical activity, the manager eagerly wants to discuss, "What are we going to do about it?" Meanwhile, the employee may not have accepted that there is a problem.

➤ *No real commitment to improve or change will occur until the employee accepts that a problem exists and it needs to be rectified.*

Without such agreement, employees and managers can spend hours in fruitless discussion. Whenever goals are not achieved as expected, the manager's primary effort must be directed at reaching a point when the staff member says, "Maybe I was at fault here. Maybe I could have done something differently."

Problems vs. Symptoms. Getting employees to accept that they have a problem only gets the manager halfway home. The question still lingers: "What is the real problem?" Rather than identifying basic causes, manager and staff members often mistake the symptoms for the problem.

For example: The deadline is passed, but an objective is still not completed (perceived problem, but actually the symptom). The manager and employee solve the problem by deciding to put some staff on overtime to get the project finished within the week.

In this case, the real problem remains unaddressed. The unasked question was, "Why was the deadline missed?" In this case, perhaps the objective was behind schedule as a result of the employee's pushy manner. In attempting to get needed data from other departments, the staff member so irritated the people concerned that they dragged their feet in supplying the information.

How to Identify the Underlying Problem. Revealing the underlying problem is difficult; sometimes it's impossible. At times, managers may experience frustration in pinpointing a basic cause because it seems that so many possibilities exist. However, we have some help for you. Only five basic causes account for most business problems. Here they are:

1. *Others/Outside Forces.* The employee works well, but external forces—for example, a death in the family or a layoff that reduced his work team— disrupt the staff member's ability to perform. The most insidious of these outside forces could

be you. It's possible—even though it's hard to admit—that you do something that hinders your staff member from accomplishing what is expected.

2. *Knowledge or Experience.* The employee needs to know more about something. (Every manager hopes this is the root cause, because remedial steps are relatively easy and safe to talk about.)

3. *Personality.* The staff member has some trait or quality that creates problems; for instance, superior attitude, impatience, aggressiveness, or stubbornness.

4. *Ability/Aptitude.* The employee lacks abilities or aptitudes for a particular kind of task; for example, poor aptitude for quantitative or conceptual thinking.

5. *Motivation.* The employee does not find satisfaction in doing something. For instance, a report is not completed because the staff member dislikes organizing details. The staff member *knows* how to organize and has the necessary *abilities.* No blocking personality *traits* and no *outside* problem interferes with the task. However, the employee does not like working with details.

You and your staff members jointly should consider each of these possibilities. This discussion can be initiated with questions such as: "Let's look at this list of possible causes. Which one do you think is at the root of the problem we're having?" or "Could the underlying problem be related to an attitude you have toward the people in sales?"

Once the basic problem has been agreed upon, remedial steps can be determined. The figure below lists the major problem areas and typical action steps that may resolve the difficulty.

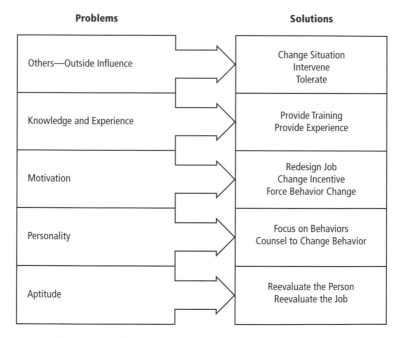

Figure 5. *Identifying problems to determine solutions*

Step 4.
Involve Employee in Determining Solutions

Involving your staff member in determining solutions is a matter of practicality and commitment. Asking the question, "What can we do about the problem?" helps. Even though the manager has a seemingly effective recommendation, the odds distinctly favor selecting the employee's approach (if both ideas have a reasonable chance of succeeding). Staff members are more likely to commit to solutions they develop.

Step 5.
Ask Employee to Summarize

Managers often report that, despite a seemingly productive discussion, staff members do not do what both sides had apparently agreed upon. The key word here is "apparently."

> ➤ *To ascertain your employees' understanding of an established course of action, ask them to summarize what happens next.*

You might ask, for instance, "Before we break up our meeting, what is your understanding of what you'll do about the problem we discussed?" Having your staff member sum up also reveals to what extent the employee has taken ownership of the problem. Most managers will be shocked at their employees' responses to this question. Often you will have to go back and reexamine if the staff member accepts that there is a problem.

Step 5 is vital to any coaching situation. It is critical that both parties leave the meeting with the same understanding of what will be done and when.

Step 6.
Set Follow-Up Date

This step is obvious, but it's also often overlooked. Before your employee leaves the progress review, a definite date should be established to discuss how things are going. Unless this date is set, meaningful change probably will not occur. Changing behavior or the manner of coping with problems is difficult. Considerable trial and error is almost always necessary before someone becomes as skillful and confident with a new approach as he or she was with the old.

> ➤ *As managers, we need to appreciate that if the employee attempts to make changes, failure should be expected more often than success. Almost all development is a process of trying and adjusting.*

The follow-up date (which could be the next scheduled progress review) should allow the staff member adequate time to try out the established change, but not so long that time is wasted if problems are encountered.

The follow-up should be structured so that the employee feels reasonably comfortable in sharing difficulties encountered while attempting to make the change. If this is not done, the staff members will not confess to failure and will simply return to the old ways. The stage can be set for an atmosphere conducive for problem solving if the manager communicates something like this:

> "Since problems could arise that neither one of us has foreseen, the changes we talked about may not work out as well in practice as we hope. Why don't you work on it between now and _____. At that time, we'll get together to see how it is going and discuss any difficulties you may be encountering."

The Follow-Up Session

If the employee has made little or no progress in implementing the desired change, perhaps:

1. The employee has not really agreed that a problem exists.

2. The problem you've been attempting to solve is not the real problem.

In such cases, you must go back to Step 2 and revisit the question, "What is the underlying problem?" Thus the change process begins anew. It is not easy.

Training Managers

In Chapter II we said that one of the primary reasons PA systems fail is that "personnel are not adequately trained to provide feedback." Proper training should enable managers to develop strong skills in performing the feedback steps described in this chapter. For any PA system to succeed, such training is absolutely essential.

➤ *Most funds allocated to the implementation of a PA system should be spent on training supervisors in how to provide negative feedback constructively and cope with their employees' defensive reactions.*

To teach coaching skills, reading materials or lecture sessions are helpful but inadequate. Learning difficult interpersonal skills requires many hands-on practice sessions with professional trainers. Such training also enhances the quality of day-to-day communication between managers and their staff.

Where We've Been; Where We're Going

This chapter offers a step-by-step procedure for providing negative feedback. Three key strategies for gaining the employee's commitment to make the desired change were suggested:

1. Avoid rejecting the employee's defensive reactions (justifying, arguing, etc.).

2. Be certain that the employee has accepted that a problem exists.

3. Be sure that your solutions address the underlying problem, not simply the symptoms.

Extensive, hands-on training of managers is essential for the success of any PA system.

The next chapter discusses step-by-step models for conducting progress reviews and summary appraisals.

IX.

THE PROGRESS REVIEW AND SUMMARY APPRAISAL

THE PERFORMANCE FEEDBACK PART of the PA system has two kinds of interviews–progress reviews and the summary appraisal. The following model shows how each should be conducted.

Progress Reviews

Progress reviews take place between the time the goals/objectives are set and the summary appraisal. How frequently progress reviews should be held depends on the job, but four to six annually is average. Quite often, monthly discussions can pay off if conditions change rapidly.

A Give-and-Take Discussion

Most progress reviews are relatively easy to conduct. They work best in a participative, "let's work together" atmosphere. The manager asks the staff member to discuss each objective, one by one, describing the degree of progress made. The manager places responsibility for providing this information on the employee's shoulders.

> *The boss should convey, in words and mannerisms, an attitude of helpfulness. In words, it might sound like this: "Let's discuss how you're doing and what problems, if any, you're encountering. Let's see if, together, we can find ways to overcome any obstacles."*

When the employee reports good progress (and the manager agrees), the manager has an opportunity to offer positive affirmation. When progress is poorer than expected, the manager initiates a problem-solving discussion with the question, "What seems to be the problem?"

A Step-by-Step Model

The progress review model consists of three simple steps:

1. Preparation

2. Review progress and reveal problems

3. Setting of next review date

Step 1–Preparation. The manager needs to organize sufficient information to know reasonably well how employees are progressing with their objectives. In organizations making extensive use of matrix management or work teams, the manager may need to consult others for relevant data, and managers should give employees a few days' notice to prepare for the review.

Step 2–Review Progress and Surface Problems. The
primary purpose of progress reviews is to help insure
that your staff's objectives get accomplished. If obstacles
hinder goal achievement, they need to be discussed. The
manager should convey that this review is not a rating
or appraisal session, but rather a time to communicate
about the employee's progress on objectives and to solve
problems.

Recognize that the manager and employee do not
have to solve every problem during the progress review.
Good judgment may dictate that some problems are best
left alone for awhile; sometimes the manager or employee
may need more time to think about the issue, and so
extended discussion is postponed.

Step 3–Set Date for Next Review. This step is obvious,
but it's mentioned because the manager should not get
locked into a prescheduled pattern of review dates. The
date selection for the next review depends on the nature
of the problems revealed. Sometimes the planned schedule
of reviews will be perfect; in other instances, significant
problems would dictate more frequent meetings.

Progress Reviews Can Be Easy, But . . . This session
is easy when employees are on track with their objectives,
or if a problem exists, employees can identify and solve it.
However, when the boss's estimation of progress differs
from that of the staff member, or if the employee does not
acknowledge apparent problems, reviews become more
difficult. In these instances, the boss must now express
disagreement with the employee's evaluation, and the

comfortable, mutual problem-solving atmosphere is apt to deteriorate.

> *To return to a problem-solving climate, the manager must respond to the employee's defenses without becoming defensive.*

This skill is so essential that all of Chapter VIII discusses this topic.

Forms for Progress Reviews

No special forms are needed. Managers may use whatever methods are most helpful for keeping track of their staff members' objectives. Some managers simply ask for a copy of each employee's list of objectives; others may want to use a simple format, such as that shown in Figure 6.

The Summary Appraisal

Employees have a right to know how the boss perceives their work. The summary appraisal provides that opportunity. It also provides a permanent record of each employee's accomplishments and failures, an important legal protection.

Timing

The appraisal is rendered at the end of the PA system's rating period. For most organizations, the appraisal is an annual event, but nothing especially recommends a 12-month cycle. Many corporations schedule the summary

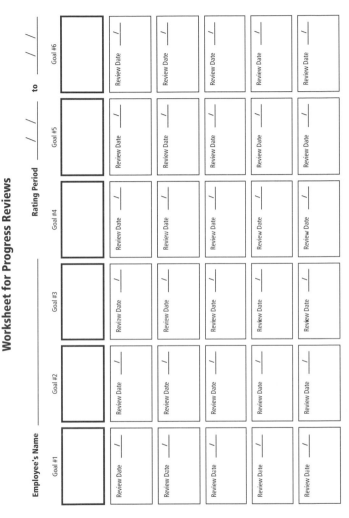

Figure 6. **Goal progress record**

appraisal close to the time that budgets are prepared for the next fiscal year. In this way, budget-related objectives for the new rating cycle are established along with other goals.

Conducting the Summary Appraisal

Summary appraisals are usually brief–not more than 30 minutes' duration. Presumably progress on all of the objectives has been discussed many times during the progress reviews, so the summary review is a brief wrap-up of the employee's work as seen through the manager's eyes.

During summary appraisals, the manager takes the lead and renders judgments. Unlike progress reviews, improvement and development are not discussed; the climate is not conducive for it.

A Step-by-Step Model

The summary appraisal model consists of four simple steps:

1. Prepare

2. Present evaluation of performance on objectives

3. Ask for employee's reactions–oral and written

4. Set stage for next round of objectives

Step 1–Prepare. As with progress reviews, the manager needs to gather data about the employee's progress. This step may require soliciting information from others with whom the employee works.

Step 2—Present Evaluation of Performance. This is the boss's chance to let employees know how their work is perceived. Since progress reviews have preceded this evaluation, the summary appraisal usually will not contain any surprises. It can be as simple as this:

Manager: Kathy, here's my written summary appraisal. As I see it, you met all of the objectives we agreed to last year, except for these two. One was to get the officewide PC system installed. I realize that you ran into problems with our supplier, and so we'll carry that project over to this year's objectives. The other project was to establish a new employee indoctrination program. As you know, that never got off the ground, and frankly, the limited effort you gave to it disappointed me. We'll need to pick that one up again and get it operational.

All in all, I think you did a good job this year managing our support group and keeping things running smoothly—especially with your downsized staff. I believe that the way you restructured your employee's jobs was the key to your success. It was an initiative that really pleased me.

Well, Kathy, that's how I saw the year. Do you have any reactions?

Step 3—Ask for Employee's Reactions. Solicit the employee's reactions both orally and in writing. The oral feedback takes place as the summary is given because the employee may have information, unknown to the manager, that might change the evaluation. The employee's written comments are recorded on the summary appraisal form immediately at the conclusion of the discussion.

The written reaction gives employees the opportunity to have their input on record. This step is important for most employees because they know that the summary appraisal could affect their future. The employee also signs off on the summary appraisal form, which protects the organization from legal action should the employee at some time claim, "I was never told."

Step 4—Set Stage for Next Round of Objectives. The summary appraisal should not be used as an occasion to establish objectives for the next rating period. However, it is a natural time to decide what to do about incomplete or unsatisfactorily performed objectives.

Where We've Been; Where We're Going

Two simple, step-by-step models—one for conducting the progress review, the other for the summary appraisal—are offered as guidelines rather than rigid formats that need to be followed. How the manager chooses to conduct these feedback sessions will depend on the employee and the boss's management style. However, in progress reviews employees should present their views first. The next chapter will focus on how to connect PA with rewards.

XYZ Corporation

Summary Appraisal
for Managerial and
Executive Personnel

Name	Title
Division or Department	Office

Accomplishments during period _____ to _____

Please check the most significant accomplishment during the period.

Accomplishments expected but not completed during period and reasons for non-completion

Figure 7.   Summary appraisal form

Considering how goals were pursued, indicate any areas for improvement

Additional comments

Form completed by

Title

Date

Duration of reporting relationship

Employee's comments

Please indicate below your reactions concerning this list of accomplishments completed and/or not completed—some expression of what to you were the most significant things achieved.

Employee's signature

Date

Figure 7.   Summary appraisal form (continued)

X.

Linking Salary to Performance

S OME PA SYSTEMS LINK goal attainment and rewards directly, usually in a mathematical formula. For example, if you get a total performance rating of "3," your salary increase is 2%; a rating of "4" yields 5%, and so on. Other mechanistic systems assign a weighting or value to each objective. These weights are then multiplied by the performance score on each respective objective and the products are then added to yield a "total performance score." This score, in turn, equates to a specific award.

The seeming objectivity of these rating formats is appealing, but they often result in both manager and employee manipulating the numbers. The employee knows that negotiating for a few more points on an objective may push the overall score to the next higher category, and hence a larger reward. The manager knows that in a direct-linkage format, only a high score justifies a high reward. Thus, the ratings communicated to the employee may be inflated, and the organization's PA records do not reflect the true level of the employee's performance.

➤ *If you want a good PA system, rewards cannot be directly linked to performance ratings.*

Salary Decisions
and Appraisal Discussions

Don't discuss salary decisions during progress reviews or summary appraisals. When money is on the line, work problems take a back seat, creating difficulty for the manager and the PA system itself. Here are three significant consequences of combining salary discussions with performance issues.

1. *Conflict and Threat.*   When money is at stake, productive discussions about performance are difficult at best, because employees perceive discussing job problems as risky. Instead, employees need to justify failures and argue for better evaluations. In this kind of climate, the likelihood of improved performance is negligible.

    Evaluation interviews connected to money also can become unpleasant and strain the manager/ employee relationship. As a result, bosses often hesitate to initiate such discussions.

2. *Skewed Evaluations.*   Managers will manipulate the evaluation so that it yields the desired rewards or salary changes and minimizes conflict with the employee.

3. *Inaccurate System.*   That is, the system fails to reflect that rewards are not based solely on

performance. At first, this may sound like heresy. In reality, however, a manager rewards employees for legitimate reasons in addition to performance. Here are some examples:

- Karen has good potential and the manager wants to keep her. At present, Karen's performance is not outstanding, but she is growing in skill and the boss wants to encourage her.

- Tim has an offer from another firm and the boss doesn't want to lose him.

- Last year, the manager implied or promised Bill that he would "take care" of him during the next round of rewards.

- Carol has some special skills or experience the boss needs or depends on. He wants to keep her on the team.

➤ *The boss may never mention these factors to the employee, but prudent organizations will recognize the importance of nonperformance issues when determining reward funding.*

Administratively Speaking

Every organization has its own system for approval of funding—especially salaries. Even so, the concepts presented here can be integrated relatively easily into current procedures. Justifying salaries should be predicated on a format that includes the following elements:

1. A section in which major achievements (objective attainments) are briefly described in one-line statements. The summary appraisal form can be substituted for this section or accompany the salary request.

2. A section headed, "Other Factors, optional." This section provides space for short paragraphs in which the manager can add justifications to the performance. These include:

    •   Critical, essential skills

    •   Pay level relative to comparable employees

    •   Past salary history

    •   Competitive demand (other job offers)

    •   Strong potential

Figure 8 shows a form for justifying a salary change. Note that the predominant emphasis is work performed, but other ancillary factors are also recognized. This justification for a salary increase is not typically shared with the employee. Usually a manager's salary recommendations and estimates of future potential remain administratively confidential.

Discussing Salary—When and How

Salary/reward discussions need to be conducted separately from the summary PA. Reward discussions are a different kind of interview—one in which the focus is not on problem solving.

Salary Change Request

Employee _____   Employee # _____

Current Position _____   Grade Level _____

Current Salary $ _____ per _____

1. Major Accomplishments (Key goals achieved or see attached copy of summary appraisal)

    a. _____

    b. _____

    c. _____

    d. _____

2. Other Considerations (Optional)

    a. Pay level relative to other comparable employees

    b. Possession of critical, essential skills

    c. Past salary treatment

    d. Potential for growth

    e. Competitive offers; marketplace competition

3. Salary Recommendation

    $ _____ per _____ Beginning _____

    Signed _____

    Job Title _____ Date _____

Figure 8.   *Salary change request*

Timing

Many believe that the reward discussion should take place close to the time of the summary or year-end PA, because managers have more data to assess the reward.

However, this timing is not critical. Job performance is typically a continuous, year-long event—objectives often carry over from one period to the next and stop and start within the evaluation cycle. Although holding reward interviews near the conclusion of a rating cycle makes sense, other considerations might dictate different practices.

What to Say

Many managers fail to realize the benefits to be derived from the reward discussion. Typically, the boss mentions the amount of the raise, the employee says, "Thanks," and that's it. Let's look at some suggestions for making more productive use of this interview.

First, the discussion can be relatively brief. In most cases, the reward is not negotiable; a decision has already been made and approved by others. For the most part, the increase represents an opportunity to reinforce good behavior and provide recognition and appreciation.

Second, solicit reactions from the employee, especially if the reward is less than the employee expected. It is better to have the employee ventilate negative feelings in the confines of your office than out among your other employees. Also, let the employee know that you understand the disappointment. Here's an example:

> *Manager:* I asked you to stop in, Bob, because I wanted to tell you how pleased I am with your performance this year. As you know, from our past discussions, you achieved most of your objectives and have made great progress in mastering this new job.

I am particularly happy about the initiative you took in setting up our budget in conjunction with the sales department.

I am also pleased with your work on the Software Task Force. When things were floundering, you exhibited strong leadership and pulled the project together. Team members have told me that your encouragement and positive attitude really helped everyone. With these thoughts in mind, I got approval of a $400 a month increase in your salary. It will be effective in your next paycheck.

Bob: Well, thank you.

Manager: I hear the "thanks," Bob, but you don't sound particularly pleased.

Bob. It's not that I don't appreciate the raise, Martha, but, well, I just thought it would be higher.

Manager: What kind of raise did you expect?

Bob: Well, I had hoped it would be $500. I know things are tight right now, so I'm really not complaining; it's good to get the $400. I just had hoped for more.

Manager: So how are you feeling about this? Are you angry or disappointed, or what?

Bob: No, I'm not angry, but I guess I am disappointed.

Manager: I hear you, Bob, and I think I understand your feelings. I just ask that you recognize that you're relatively new to this job and, while you've done well, there's still lots of room for growth.

Bob: I realize that. And thank you for listening . . . actually I feel pretty good right now.

The Key Ingredients in the Reward Discussion Are:
1. Praise and recognition for accomplishments
2. The amount of the reward, stated without equivocation
3. Opportunity for employee to express reactions

Where We've Been; Where We're Going

This chapter pointed out several problems that result from directly linking rewards with job performance. Rewards should be primarily based on performance, but not mechanistically. In reality, other factors, such as potential, also need to be factored in. Managers also should separate PA discussions from reward discussions. Failure to do so probably will result in little or no work improvement, erroneous evaluations, strained boss-employee relationships, and resistance to the PA system.

Good reward interviews provide recognition for a job well done, reinforcement of good behavior, and a brief, unequivocal statement of the reward. Give employees an opportunity to voice their reactions.

The next chapter will discuss how the PA system proposed here can help with promotion and legal issues.

XI.

PROMOTIONS AND
LEGAL ISSUES

A T THE BEGINNING OF THIS BOOK we said that a PA system rarely can both improve performance and be useful for determining salary increases and promotions. That statement is true. However, by separating performance discussions from salary awards, managers can combine the two in a single PA system. The same concept applies to promotions.

Most designers of PA systems believe that they need a categorical or overall rating score to make PA helpful for promotion or salary decisions. No such rating is provided on the summary appraisal form, which nonetheless provides a sound basis for reward recommendations. Similarly, the summary appraisal can provide the ideal input for making promotional decisions.

Experienced managers know that overall ratings of potential such as "Limited," "Average," or "Above Average" can be deceptive when they attempt to select a candidate for promotion. In PA systems that use overall or quantitative ratings, the ratings are almost always skewed to the high side. Such ratings can lead to poor decisions if managers rely on them for promotional purposes.

The PA system proposed here has no overall or quantitative ratings. Instead, the summary appraisal form describes all of the major goals the candidate did or did not accomplish. If you have the candidate's summary appraisals for several years, you have a clear picture of the kind of work the candidate can do.

The PA system and summary appraisal described here provide an excellent basis for defense in case of alleged discrimination. If an employee does not deserve promotion because of limited ability or poor job performance, employers can usually establish this fact by pointing to the "noncompleted goals" or the limited value of those accomplished. Since employees write their reaction to the appraisal as well as sign off on it, employers have proof that employees were informed about their performance.

Of course, the converse is also true. The PA system and summary appraisal also reveal good performance.

Where We've Been; Where We're Going

This chapter has demonstrated how the completed summary appraisal provides a sound source of data for helping to make promotion decisions. The same form also provides strong source information for defense against charges of discrimination.

This book attempts to define a PA system that works—one that improves performance and that managers find useful. May you have much success with it.

FURTHER READING

DeVries, David L., Ann M. Morrison, Sandra L. Shullman, and Michael L. Gerlach. *Performance Appraisal on the Line.* New York: John Wiley & Sons, 1981.

Drake, John D. *The Effective Interviewer.* New York: AMACOM, 1989.

Edwards, Mark R. and Ann J. Ewen. *360° Feedback.* New York: AMACOM, 1996.

McGregor, D. "An Uneasy Look at Performance Appraisal," *Harvard Business Review* Vol. 35 No. 3: (1957) 89–94.

Meyer, H. H., E. Kay, and J. R. P. French. "Split Roles in Performance Appraisal." *Harvard Business Review* Vol. 43 No. 1: (1965) 123–129.

About the Author

John D. Drake serves as board chairman of Drake Inglesi Milardo, Inc., a human resources consulting firm that he founded. Before establishing this company, he started and was CEO of Drake Beam & Associates, Inc. (now Drake Beam Morin, Inc.), the world's largest outplacement firm with more than 200 offices in 37 countries. Drake earned his Ph.D. in counseling psychology from Case Western Reserve University in Cleveland, Ohio. He has written several books, including *The Effective Interviewer*, a management best-seller. Other published titles include *The Perfect Interview: How to Get the Job You Really Want, A CEO's Guide to Interpersonal Relations,* and *Counseling Techniques for the Non-Personnel Executive.* His new book, *Work Time, Play Time—Finding the Perfect Balance,* is forthcoming. He can be reached at P.O. Box 1516, Kennebunkport, ME 04046; e-mail Drake5546@aol.com.